A PEARL HARBOR TIME CAPSULE

ARTIFACTS OF THE SURPRISE ATTACK ON THE U.S.

by Natalie Fowler

Consultant:
Richard Bell, PhD
Associate Professor of History
University of Maryland, College Park

CAPSTONE PRESS
a capstone imprint

Capstone Captivate is published by Capstone Press, an imprint of Capstone.
1710 Roe Crest Drive
North Mankato, Minnesota 56003
www.capstonepub.com

Library of Congress Cataloging-in-Publication Data is available on the Library of Congress website.
ISBN: 978-1-5435-9232-0 (library binding)
ISBN: 978-1-4966-6630-7 (paperback)
ISBN: 978-1-5435-9239-9 (eBook pdf)

Summary: A Japanese war map, a midget submarine, and evacuation orders are all part of the story of Japan's surprise attack on Pearl Harbor on December 7, 1941. By examining these and other artifacts, readers feel like they are witnesses to the attack that brought the United States into World War II. Open this imaginary time capsule and learn!

Image Credits
Alamy: FLHC A17, 16; DVIC: NARA, 12, 31, 41, 43; Getty Images: Bettmann, 32, Popperfoto/Paul Popper, 36, The LIFE Picture Collection/Life Magazine/Ralph Morse, 37, ullstein bild Dtl., 8; Library of Congress: 5, 22; National Park Service: Pearl Harbor National Memorial, 14, 28; Newscom: akg-images, 21, Everett Collection, 7, Photoshot/UPPA, 18; Shutterstock: ale-kup (background), cover and throughout, Dan Gor, 23, pinggr, cover (top right), Pung, 29, Reuben Teo, 6, sutham, 10; U.S. National Archives: 30, 34, 38; U.S. Naval History and Heritage Command: cover (left), 24, U.S. National Archives, cover (middle), U.S. Navy, 19; Wikimedia: World Imaging, 42; XNR Productions, 26

Editorial Credits
Editor: Julie Gassman; Designer: Lori Bye; Media Researcher: Svetlana Zhurkin; Production Specialist: Tori Abraham

All internet sites appearing in back matter were available and accurate when this book was sent to press.

Printed in the United States of America.
PA117

Table of Contents

Words in **bold** are in the glossary.

CHAPTER 1
INTRODUCTION

When something important happens, we want to remember it. One of the ways we can do that is to save special things from that event. Artifacts such as historical maps, photographs, and equipment can be evidence that helps to prove what happened and show how people reacted. This collection of items could even be kept in a time capsule—a container of artifacts buried away for discovery in the future.

What if there were a special time capsule for each important moment in history? What if you found one of these time capsules? What might be in it?

In 1941, much of the world was at war. Germany, led by Adolf Hitler, was taking over Europe. In Asia, Japan was at war with China.

The United States had troops stationed at Pearl Harbor in Hawaii to protect its interests in the South Pacific. On December 7, 1941, Japan attacked the United States by bombing Pearl Harbor. This surprise attack was the reason the United States entered World War II (1939–1945). If this historic day had its own time capsule, what would be in it?

Japan targeted U.S. battleships in the attack on Pearl Harbor.

CHAPTER 2

JAPAN AT WAR

From the Time Capsule: LION FROM THE MARCO POLO BRIDGE

TIME CAPSULE
ARTIFACT:
STONE LION

Opening up our imaginary time capsule, you might see that the first item is a lion, carved out of stone. It comes from an important bridge in China, just outside of the city of Beijing. This bridge is called Lugou Bridge in China and the Marco Polo Bridge elsewhere.

In 1926, Hirohito became emperor of Japan. Emperor Hirohito used his powerful military to attack neighboring countries. In 1931, the Japanese army took over Manchuria in northeastern China. On July 7, 1937, the Chinese successfully defended themselves against the Japanese on the Marco Polo Bridge. But their victory didn't last long. Japan invaded and occupied the city of Beijing.

Emperor Hirohito

Japanese troops entered a city in Manchuria after the army took over that region in China.

The battle on the Marco Polo Bridge became known as the "Marco Polo Bridge Incident." It is considered by some to be the beginning of World War II in Asia.

When looking at the timeline and history of Japan's quest to conquer China and other territories in Asia, questions come to mind. Why? What did Japan want? Why did Japan want to take over China?

Japan is an island country that has very few **natural resources**. All around, other countries were developing **technology** and gaining wealth and power because they had natural resources that other countries wanted. Also, because Japan is an island, its land was limited. Japan wanted to take over China so it could become a larger, more powerful nation.

Fact

After World War I, the **League of Nations** was created to help countries work together to solve problems and prevent wars. Japan was a founding member. In 1933, Japan was criticized by the League of Nations for its attack on Manchuria, so Japan withdrew from the League of Nations.

From the Time Capsule:
SAMPLE OF RUBBER

TIME CAPSULE ARTIFACT: RUBBER

If you looked into our time capsule again, the next item you might see is a strange white, rounded chunk. This substance came from a rubber tree. Rubber was a resource that Japan needed but didn't have. Oil was another one of the most important resources Japan needed to make advancements and improvements in its technology.

Most of the natural resources in Southeast Asia came from other Asian countries. Some of them were controlled by Western countries as colonies. For example, oil was available in Indonesia, a Dutch colony. Rubber was found in the British colony, Malaysia.

Oil was necessary for fuel. Rubber was needed to make all sorts of things, from tires to waterproof shoes. Even more important, rubber was needed for many of the products used in war, such as wheels for tanks and parts for submarines. It was even wrapped around wires.

At the time, other countries in Southeast Asia produced the majority of the world's rubber. Whoever controlled these countries could control the production of a resource everyone in the world needed and wanted, especially during a war. Japan wanted to control these resources. It also didn't want to have to depend on other countries to get these resources for itself.

From the Time Capsule:
INFAMOUS "BLOODY SATURDAY" PHOTO

TIME CAPSULE ARTIFACT:
"BLOODY SATURDAY" PHOTO

If you looked into our time capsule for the next item, your eyes might settle on a photograph of a baby crying. It can be a difficult photo to look at, but it is a very important picture.

The photo was taken immediately after Japan attacked the Chinese city of Shanghai on August 28, 1937. This famous picture by Chinese photographer H.S. Wong of a wounded, helpless baby was sent to a New York City newspaper and eventually viewed by an estimated 136 million people.

Many Chinese citizens were killed when Japan invaded their cities. After people around the world saw this photo, they realized that innocent people, even babies, were victims.

Less than a month before the surprise attack, battleships sat in a line along the shore of Ford Island at Pearl Harbor.

In order to make Japan realize it couldn't just take what it wanted, the U.S. government refused to trade goods and services with Japan. But Japan became more determined than ever to stand its ground.

The United States stationed bomber planes and ships in the South Pacific. It was a warning to Japan that the Americans were willing to defend their South Pacific colonies, including Guam, the Philippines, and Hawaii. On the Hawaiian island of Oahu, the Hickam Air Force Base was home to the U.S. Air Force and the Naval Station Pearl Harbor was the home base for U.S. naval battleships.

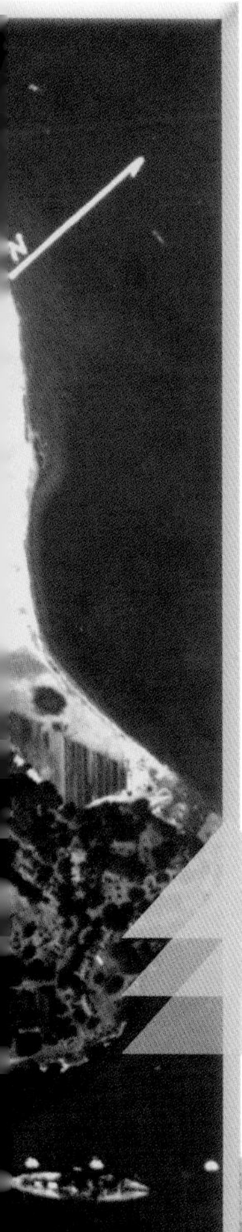

CHAPTER 3
THE AXIS POWERS

From the Time Capsule:
JAPANESE POSTER

TIME CAPSULE ARTIFACT:
JAPANESE POSTER

The next item in our time capsule might be a little tattered. Perhaps when you pull it out, you have to be careful not to rip it. It is a Japanese poster showing three women from three countries, each holding up a picture of a different leader. These leaders were from Germany, Japan, and Italy. These three countries became known as the Axis powers.

Adolf Hitler was a leader who rose to power in Germany at a time when the world was still recovering from World War I (1914–1918). His supporters were known as Nazis. He began to secretly build up the German army.

Hitler withdrew Germany from the League of Nations and started taking over other countries in Europe.

The agreement between Germany, Italy, and Japan was called the Tripartite Pact.

In October 1936, Hitler agreed to work with Benito Mussolini, the **fascist** leader of Italy. In September 1939, Britain and France declared war on Germany. By the end of 1939, most of Europe was at war.

In September 1940, Japan joined Germany and Italy and all three countries agreed to work together. They decided that an attack or a declaration of war against one of their countries would be considered an attack against all.

From the Time Capsule: JAPANESE STRATEGIC ATTACK MAP

TIME CAPSULE ARTIFACT: ATTACK MAP

As you pull out the next item, you realize that it is a map. But you might not be able to read the writing on it. This is an important, rare map—with Japanese writing—that was used by the Japanese navy when it planned the attack on Pearl Harbor.

After Japan's attack and occupation of Manchuria, the United States hoped that the limitations on trade with Japan would encourage Japan to stop its aggressive plan to expand. But Japan resented that the United States supported China and was interfering with anything going on in Asia.

The United States and Japan attempted to negotiate a peaceful end to the trade limitations. In November 1941, Japan presented a proposal to the United States, offering to partially withdraw its troops from China. The United States rejected this proposal. Japan offered a final proposal that required the United States to supply Japan with oil.

The United States considered this proposal until it learned that Japan was sending more troops to French Indochina, which they had invaded in late September 1940. Instead, the United States demanded that Japan leave French Indochina and China.

The negotiations to ease tensions between Japan and the United States took place in Washington, D.C., just three weeks before the attack on Pearl Harbor.

Fact

In 1940, when Nazi Germany took over France, Japan saw an opportunity to invade the French colony of Indochina. Japan invaded French Indochina on September 22, 1940, and by September 26 occupied the territory.

The only option Japanese rulers saw was to go to war. Japanese Admiral Isoroku Yamamoto was commander in chief of Japan's navy and planned the attack on Pearl Harbor. Because there were so many American soldiers stationed at Pearl Harbor, he knew it was extremely important to keep the attack a surprise.

Admiral Isoroku Yamamoto

Hawaii was 4,000 miles (6,437 kilometers) away from Japan. In order to organize a sneak attack on a location that far away, Japan had to move its airplanes and submarines to the right location without being detected. For several months, the Japanese military planned its attack and practiced its plan over and over again.

CHAPTER 4

JAPAN'S ATTACK

From the Time Capsule: JAPANESE MITSUBISHI A6M ZERO FIGHTER PLANE

TIME CAPSULE ARTIFACT: FIGHTER PLANE

You might be surprised by how large the next item in our time capsule is. It's a Japanese airplane—the Mitsubishi A6M Zero fighter plane. These fighter planes worked with bombers to attack Hickam airfield, so that U.S. fighter planes would not be able to take off. This plane was fast and efficient. It was the best fighter airplane at the time of the attack on Pearl Harbor.

At 7:02 a.m., a **radar** station (Opana Point on Oahu) detected a signal. The signal told the operators in the tower that a large number of planes was approaching. But radar was a new technology. Also, a large group of planes was expected from California that same morning. The operators didn't realize they were seeing enemy planes on their radar.

From the Time Capsule:
MIDGET SUBMARINE

TIME CAPSULE ARTIFACT:
MIDGET SUBMARINE

A Japanese fighter plane is not the only military vehicles you will discover. Next time you peek over the edge of our time capsule, you might see a small submarine! Before the attack on Pearl Harbor even began, these midget submarines were already lurking underwater.

Normal submarines can carry a crew of more than 100 people. These miniature versions of submarines carried only two crew members and two torpedoes. But those torpedoes had double the explosive power of the Japanese bombers. The midget submarines could also move easily into shallow waters. They were able to sneak into Pearl Harbor undetected.

Attack Details

- At 7:55 a.m. on December 7, alarm bells rang on the USS *West Virginia*.
- On the USS *Arizona*, a bomb hit its ammunition storage and the ship exploded, killing 1,177 officers, sailors, and Marines.
- The USS *Oklahoma* rolled after it was hit, trapping 400 crew members. Oil spilled out of it and caught fire, burning those trying to swim toward safety.

From the Time Capsule:
ELGIN CLOCK

TIME CAPSULE ARTIFACT: CLOCK

The next item in our time capsule is a clock. This is a clock that was recovered from the sunken wreckage of the gigantic battleship, the USS *Arizona.* This item in our time capsule represents all the death and destruction that happened on that fateful day.

The USS *Arizona* was one of eight battleships damaged during the attack on Pearl Harbor. It was hit by four bombs and sank to the bottom of the harbor. Almost half of the victims at Pearl Harbor were from the USS *Arizona*, with its 1,177 crew members killed.

The USS *Arizona* Memorial sits over the sunken ship, marking the resting place of more than 900 sailors and Marines.

Fact

Most of the crew members killed on the USS *Arizona* remained with their ship. It was too difficult to get their bodies out of the wreckage.

CHAPTER 5
WAR ON JAPAN

From the Time Capsule:
SPEECH TO CONGRESS

The next time capsule item might not look like anything important—just some papers with scribbles and crossed-out words. But it's the draft of President Franklin D. Roosevelt's famous speech to Congress, in which he asked Congress to declare war on Japan.

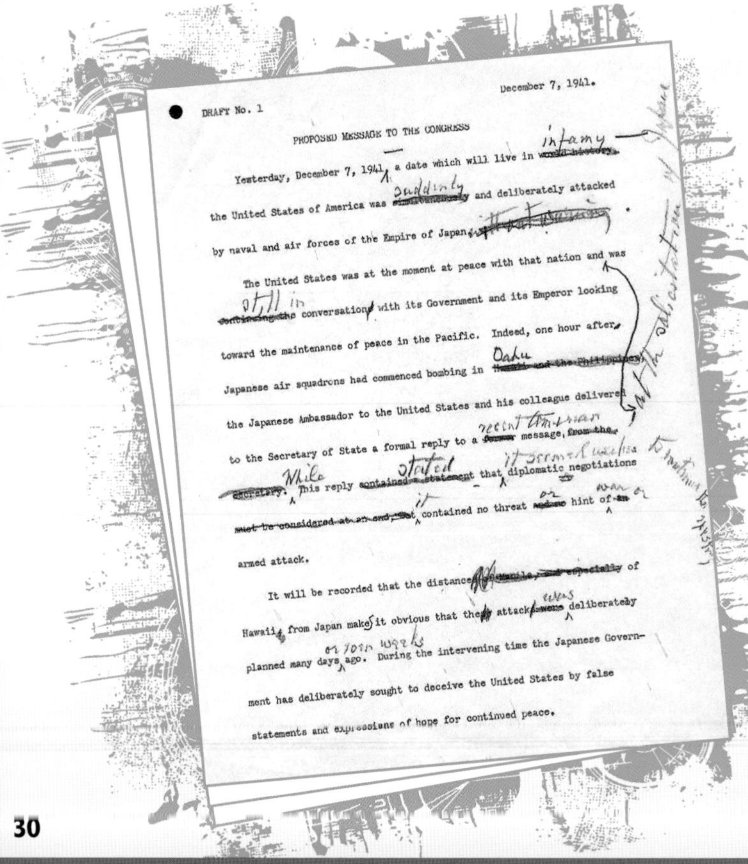

DRAFT No. 1

December 7, 1941.

PROPOSED MESSAGE TO THE CONGRESS

Yesterday, December 7, 1941, a date which will live in world history, the United States of America was simultaneously and deliberately attacked by naval and air forces of the Empire of Japan.

The United States was at the moment at peace with that nation and was continuing the conversations with its Government and its Emperor looking toward the maintenance of peace in the Pacific. Indeed, one hour after Japanese air squadrons had commenced bombing in Hawaii and the Philippines, the Japanese Ambassador to the United States and his colleague delivered to the Secretary of State a formal reply to a former message, from the Secretary. This reply contained a statement that diplomatic negotiations must be considered at an end, but contained no threat and no hint of an armed attack.

It will be recorded that the distance of Manila, and especially of Hawaii, from Japan make it obvious that these attacks were deliberately planned many days ago. During the intervening time the Japanese Government has deliberately sought to deceive the United States by false statements and expressions of hope for continued peace.

TIME CAPSULE ARTIFACT:
PRESIDENT'S SPEECH

On December 7, 1941, President Roosevelt was just finishing his lunch in Washington, D.C., when he received the first report about the attack on Pearl Harbor. He decided to go before Congress the next day and ask for a declaration of war.

As Roosevelt worked on his speech, one of the changes he made was to change the words “a date which will live in world history” to “a date which will live in **infamy**.” It became one of the most famous lines from his speech.

Less than an hour after President Roosevelt gave his speech, Congress agreed to declare war on Japan.

President Roosevelt signed a declaration of war against Japan on December 8, 1941.

From the Time Capsule:

NEWSPAPER ANNOUNCING THE ATTACK

"All the News That's Fit to Print."

The New York Times.

LATE CITY EDITION

NEW YORK, MONDAY, DECEMBER 8, 1941.

THREE CENTS

JAPAN WARS ON U. S. AND BRITAIN; MAKES SUDDEN ATTACK ON HAWAII; HEAVY FIGHTING AT SEA REPORTED

CONGRESS DECIDED

Roosevelt Will Address It Today and Find It Ready to Vote War

CONFERENCE IS HELD

Legislative Leaders and Cabinet in Sober White House Talk

By C. P. TRUSSELL

TOKYO ACTS FIRST

Declaration Follows Air and Sea Attacks on U. S. and Britain

TOGO CALLS ENVOYS

After Fighting Is On, Grew Gets Japan's Reply to Hull Note of Nov. 26

By The Associated Press.

PACIFIC OCEAN: THEATRE OF WAR INVOLVING UNITED STATES AND ITS ALLIES

GUAM BOMBED; ARMY SHIP IS SUNK

U. S. Fliers Head North From Manila—Battleship Oklahoma Set Afire by Torpedo Planes at Honolulu

104 SOLDIERS KILLED AT FIELD IN HAWAII

Japanese Envoys, at Moment of Attack, Deliver Reply to U. S. Note—President Sees Cabinet and Drafts Message to Congress

By FRANK L. KLUCKHOHN

WASHINGTON, Monday, Dec. 8—Sudden and unexpected attacks on Pearl Harbor, Honolulu, and other United States possessions in the Pacific early yesterday by the Japanese air force and navy plunged the United States and Japan into active war.

The initial attack in Hawaii, apparently launched by torpedo-carrying bombers and submarines, caused widespread damage and death. It was quickly followed by others. There were unconfirmed reports that German raiders participated in the attacks.

Guam also was assaulted from the air, as were Davao, on the island of Mindanao, and Camp John Hayes, in Northern Luzon.

TIME CAPSULE ARTIFACT: NEWSPAPER

If you were to reach into the time capsule again, you might pull out a tattered old copy of *The New York Times.* In the 1940s, reading newspapers was one of the most important ways people learned about what was going on in the world.

As people read their newspapers in the days after the attack on Pearl Harbor, they learned their country was at war.

On December 11, Germany and Italy declared war on the United States in response to the U.S. declaration of war on Japan. The United States responded the same day by declaring war on Germany and Italy.

Other countries were already working together to fight the Axis powers. The group of countries that joined others to fight against the Axis powers became known as the Allied powers. These countries included Great Britain, France, China, and the Soviet Union. When the United States entered the war, it became one of the Allied powers.

From the Time Capsule:
U.S. ARMY POSTER

TIME CAPSULE ARTIFACT:
PROPAGANDA POSTER

If you were to pull out more paper from the time capsule, you might think it needs to go into the recycling bin. But don't throw it away! It is an advertisement from the U.S. government encouraging people to support the war effort.

Fighting a war takes a big commitment from everyone in the country. Families were sending their loved ones off to fight in the war, and people everywhere had to help however they could.

The government worked hard to encourage support by making signs and banners to remind people why it was important to fight. **Propaganda** was everywhere, and many posters, banners, and buttons asked people to "Remember Pearl Harbor."

Fact

To this day, collectors all over the world are interested in objects from World War II, especially propaganda items.

From the Time Capsule:

PHOTO OF WAIKIKI DURING WARTIME

As you reach into the time capsule to pull out our next item, you might be looking at a photograph that never should have been taken in the first place. After the attack, no one was allowed to take photographs in Hawaii. The U.S. government was afraid that photos might end up in enemy hands. This picture, with barbed wire lining the beach, represents how much life changed in Hawaii after the bombing of Pearl Harbor.

TIME CAPSULE ARTIFACT:
WAIKIKI BEACH PHOTO

After the United States went to war with Japan, **martial law** was declared in Hawaii. Everyday life in Hawaii, including its most important industry, tourism, came to an end. Everyone was forced to obey strict rules.

Barbed wire was put around all of the beaches. Residents had to live with a **curfew**. Without a pass, anyone out after dark could be arrested. Life in Hawaii continued under martial law until October 24, 1944.

Blackout rules were part of martial law in Hawaii, making it harder for Japanese bombers to find targets.

From the Time Capsule:

EXECUTIVE ORDERS 9066 AND 9102

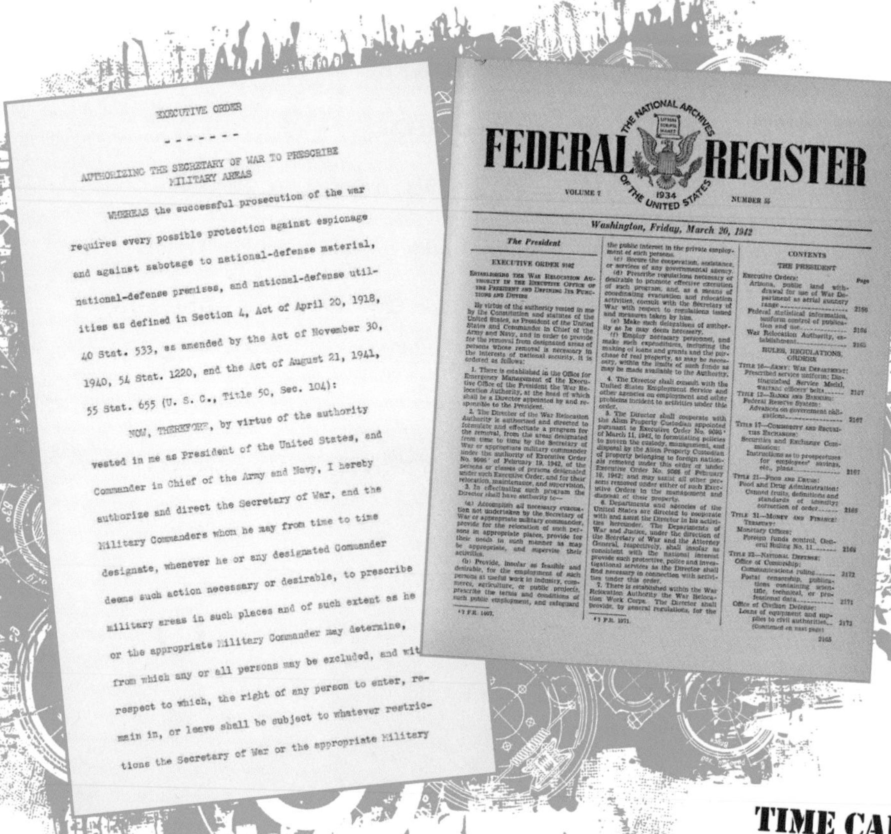
EXECUTIVE ORDER

- - - - - - -

AUTHORIZING THE SECRETARY OF WAR TO PRESCRIBE MILITARY AREAS

WHEREAS the successful prosecution of the war requires every possible protection against espionage and against sabotage to national-defense material, national-defense premises, and national-defense util- ities as defined in Section 4, Act of April 20, 1918, 40 Stat. 533, as amended by the Act of November 30, 1940, 54 Stat. 1220, and the Act of August 21, 1941, 55 Stat. 655 (U. S. C., Title 50, Sec. 104):

NOW, THEREFORE, by virtue of the authority vested in me as President of the United States, and Commander in Chief of the Army and Navy, I hereby authorize and direct the Secretary of War, and the Military Commanders whom he may from time to time designate, whenever he or any designated Commander deems such action necessary or desirable, to prescribe military areas in such places and of such extent as he or the appropriate Military Commander may determine, from which any or all persons may be excluded, and wit respect to which, the right of any person to enter, re- main in, or leave shall be subject to whatever restric- tions the Secretary of War or the appropriate Military

FEDERAL REGISTER

THE NATIONAL ARCHIVES OF THE UNITED STATES 1934

VOLUME 7 NUMBER 55

Washington, Friday, March 20, 1942

The President

EXECUTIVE ORDER 9102

CONTENTS

THE PRESIDENT

TIME CAPSULE ARTIFACTS: EXECUTIVE ORDERS

As you peer into the time capsule, another pair of documents catches your attention. These documents are **executive orders** from President Roosevelt.

On February 19, 1942, President Roosevelt signed Executive Order 9066, giving the military the authority to exclude "any or all persons from designated areas, including the California coast." About a month later, Roosevelt signed Executive Order 9102 to establish the War Relocation Authority.

These orders meant that Japanese American citizens were not trusted and forced to go to places called internment camps until further notice. They lost their property, and many people permanently lost their jobs.

Executive Orders 9066 and 9102 have since been declared a major violation of Japanese Americans' **civil rights**. Japanese Americans were treated unfairly by their government simply because of their race.

Fact

The internment camps were surrounded by barbed-wire fences. Guards were instructed to shoot anyone who tried to escape.

CHAPTER 6

THE END OF WORLD WAR II

The Americans fought a bloody battle against Japan in the South Pacific. Later in the war, the Japanese used suicide pilots, who crashed their planes into Allied targets. At the same time, the United States was also supporting the Allied forces in Europe.

The United States knew that if it tried to invade Japan, it would suffer horrible loss of life. In the attempt to bring the war to an end sooner, on August 6, 1945, it dropped a newly developed **atomic bomb** on the Japanese city of Hiroshima. The powerful bomb destroyed the city and killed thousands of people. Despite this terrible show of force, the Japanese did not surrender.

Three days later, on August 9, the United States dropped yet another atomic bomb, this time on the Japanese city of Nagasaki, destroying that city and killing tens of thousands more people.

Historians estimate between 60,000 and 80,000 people died from the bombing of Nagasaki.

From the Time Capsule:
SURRENDER PAPERS

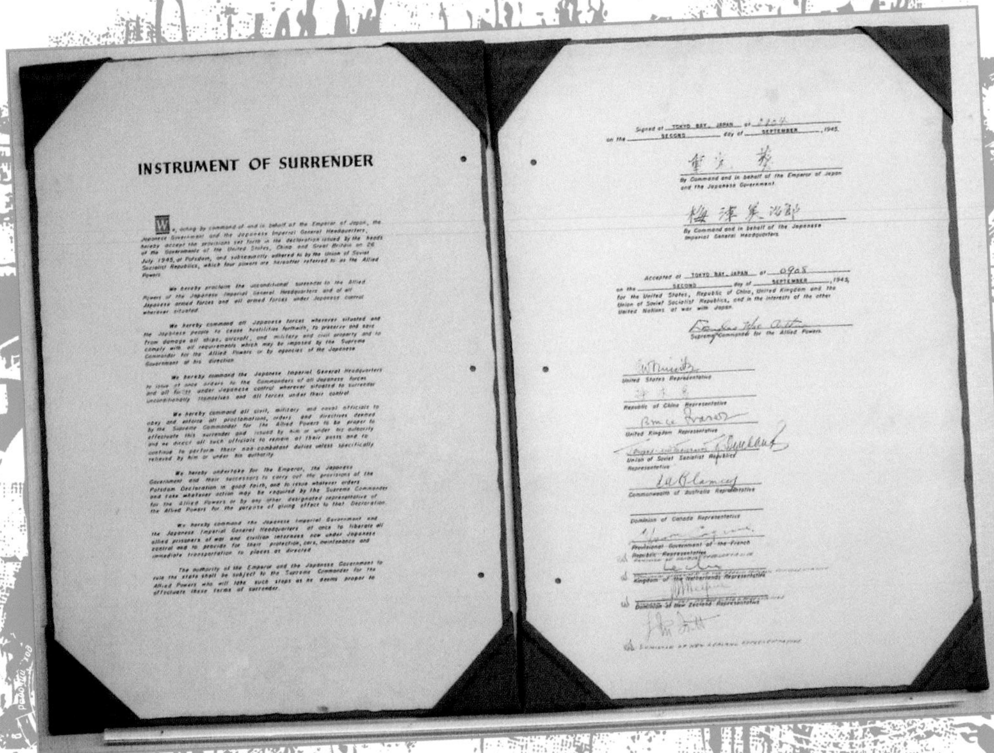

TIME CAPSULE
ARTIFACT:
SURRENDER PAPERS

Imagine looking into the time capsule and seeing just one item remaining—a folder of sorts. As you open it, you will see some very important signatures.

This signed agreement represents the end of World War II. Japan finally surrendered on August 15, 1945. On September 2, 1945, representatives of Japan and the United States signed these formal surrender papers aboard the USS *Missouri* in Tokyo Bay.

Now imagine all of the time capsule items spread out in front of us. Can you see how each artifact adds an important piece to the story? By looking at them all together, we can better understand how the attack on Pearl Harbor changed the course of history.

Supreme Allied Commander, U.S. General Douglas MacArthur, signed the surrender papers during the formal ceremony aboard the USS *Missouri*.

More About the Artifacts

Lion from the Marco Polo Bridge

Made of granite, the bridge stretches over the Yongding River in China, just outside of Beijing.

Sample of Rubber

Rubber is collected from trees in the same way syrup is collected from maple trees. Cuts are made in the tree trunk, and the white sap drips out into a bucket. The sap (liquid rubber) is heated over a fire and thickened into a ball shape.

Infamous "Bloody Saturday" Photo

"Bloody Saturday," photographed by Chinese photographer H.S. Wong, has been named as one of the most powerful news images of all time and included as one of *Time* magazine's 100 most influential photos.

Japanese Poster

In this Japanese poster, there are three young women. One is holding a stick with the image of Adolf Hitler and a swastika, the symbol for the Nazi political party. Another is holding up the image of Hideki Tōjō, the imperialist leader of Japan during World War II. The third is holding up the image of Benito Mussolini, the fascist leader of Italy.

Japanese Strategic Attack Map

This map was recovered from a Japanese aircraft that was shot down during the Pearl Harbor attack. It shows where the U.S. ships, aircraft carriers, and battleships were supposed to be parked. Now, this artifact is part of the U.S. National Archives collection.

Japanese Mitsubishi A6M Zero Fighter Plane

The Japanese Mitsubishi A6M Zero fighter plane was known for its great maneuverability and ability to fly long distances. This restored fighter plane is now on display at the Japan Air Self-Defense Force Museum in Hamamatsu, Japan.

Midget Submarine

This Japanese midget submarine was discovered on December 8, 1941, the day after the attack on Pearl Harbor, and salvaged by U.S. forces.

Elgin Clock

This Elgin brand clock was recovered from the wreckage of the USS Arizona after it sank during the bombing of Pearl Harbor. This artifact has been preserved by the U.S. National Park Service.

Speech to Congress

This speech by Roosevelt became known as the "Day of Infamy Speech" because of its first line, in which he stated that the bombing of Pearl Harbor would be a "date which will live in infamy." The draft is kept in the U.S. National Archives.

Newspaper Announcing the Attack

On December 8, 1941, the headlines of newspapers everywhere shouted that Japan had attacked Pearl Harbor. These headlines made it clear that the U.S. could no longer avoid entering World War II.

U.S. Army Poster

As a way to encourage and inspire Americans to make it through the sacrifice of war, propaganda posters and buttons with slogans were distributed everywhere. This poster, "Avenge Pearl Harbor," was from 1942 or 1943.

Photo of Waikiki During Wartime

During the war, the U.S. government forbade taking photos like this one because it did not want records of landscape and methods of defense (barbed wire) to end up in enemy hands.

Executive Orders 9066 and 9102

President Roosevelt signed Executive Order 9066 on February 19, 1942. This order allowed the removal of people from military areas. The order defined the entire West Coast, home to many Japanese families, as a military area. Executive Order 9102 created the War Relocation Authority on March 18, 1942. The War Relocation Authority had the power to enforce Executive Order 9066. Because of these executive orders, many Japanese Americans were forced to live in internment camps.

Surrender Papers

Entitled "Instrument of Surrender," this document officially ended the United States' war with Japan. A 23-minute ceremony was held on board the USS *Missouri* on September 2, 1945, and was broadcast on radio around the world. At 9:08 a.m., the United States accepted the surrender on behalf of the Allied powers.

Glossary

atomic bomb (uh-TOM-ik BOM)—a powerful bomb that explodes with great force; atomic bombs destroy large areas and leave behind dangerous radiation

civil rights (SI-vil RYTS)—the rights that all people have to freedom and equal treatment under the law

curfew (KUR-fyoo)—a rule requiring that everyone be off the street and inside their homes at a certain time

executive order (ig-ZE-kyuh-tiv OR-der)—proclamation by a president that has the force of law

fascist (FASH-ist)—having complete power and control

infamy (IN-fuh-mee)—the state of being well-known for evil

League of Nations (LEEG UHV NAY-shuhns)—a political organization established after World War I so countries could work together to solve different world issues

martial law (MAR-shuhl LAW)—control of people by the government's military instead of by civilian forces, often during an emergency

natural resources (NACH-ur-uhl REE-sors-es)—materials found in nature that people use

propaganda (prop-uh-GAN-duh)—information spread to try to influence the thinking of people; often not completely true

radar (RAY-dar)—a system that uses high-frequency sound waves to detect the presence of aircraft, vehicles, or ships

technology (tek-NOL-uh-jee)—the use of science to do practical things, such as designing complex machines

Read More

Bodden, Valerie. *The Attack on Pearl Harbor.* Mankato, MN: Creative Education, 2018.

Poe, Mayumi Shimose. *Alice on the Island: A Pearl Harbor Survival Story.* North Mankato, MN: Stone Arch Books, 2019.

Waxman, Laura Hamilton. *Japanese American Internment Camps.* Minneapolis: Lerner, 2018.

Internet Sites

American Historama: Pearl Harbor Facts
http://www.american-historama.org/1929-1945-depression-ww2-era/pearl-harbor-facts.htm

History for Kids: Pearl Harbor
http://www.historyforkids.net/pearl-harbor.html

National Geographic Kids: Attack on Pearl Harbor
https://kids.nationalgeographic.com/explore/history/pearl-harbor/

Index